To Po

Christmas 96
WWCE

To Pat

Christmas 96

Love E.

IN MY TENT

by **Marilyn Singer**
illustrated by **Emily Arnold McCully**

Macmillan Publishing Company   New York

Maxwell Macmillan Canada   Toronto

Maxwell Macmillan International   New York Oxford Singapore Sydney

Thanks to Steve Aronson, Elly Kover, Terry Moogan,
and especially Judy Whipple.

Macmillan Publishing Company is part of the Maxwell Communications Group of Companies.
Macmillan Publishing Company, 866 Third Avenue, New York, NY 10022.
Maxwell Macmillan Canada, Inc., 1200 Eglinton Avenue East, Suite 200, Don Mills, Ontario M3C 3N1.
First edition
Printed in Hong Kong
1   3   5   7   9   10   8   6   4   2
The text of this book is set in 12 pt. Adroit Light.
The illustrations are rendered in watercolor.

Library of Congress Cataloging-in-Publication Data
Singer, Marilyn.
In my tent / by Marilyn Singer ; illustrated by Emily Arnold McCully. – 1st ed.
p.   cm.
Summary: A series of poems about a little girl's first camping trip.
ISBN 0-02-782701-1
1. Camping – Juvenile poetry. 2. Children's poetry, American. [1. Camping – Poetry.]
I. McCully, Emily Arnold. ill. II. Title.
PS3569.I546I5   1992   813'.54–dc20   [E]   91-16115

To Kathleen Cotter.
    —M.S.

On the day the twins were born
Dad promised me
    my very own tent
The snow was falling in fat flakes
    on the river
        like feathers from my pillow
        when I have a fight with Jon
It was hard to think of sleeping
    under the stars
        with the tricky wind tickling our noses
                nibbling our ears
But Dad bent his head
    to the frozen ground
"Listen hard," he said
      "and you can hear spring snoring"
So I bent too
    and listened
    and heard a tiny *puh puh puh*
      gentle as a baby's breath
"She'll be getting up soon," Dad said
But we tiptoed all the way home
    so she wouldn't wake up yet

Dad says my tent is rugged
    a bear's claws could not tear it apart
Mom thinks the zippers are nifty
    opening flaps to the fresh morning air
Jon's favorite thing is the size
    big enough for a full-grown man
    or a half-grown kid with a dog at his feet
But what I like best is the color
    suddenly orange
      like an oriole landing
      in the emerald woods
        quietly saying, I'm here

Packing the car we play
Guess the Twins' First Word
"Work," Mom suggests,
        hoisting the stubborn green stove
        into the trunk
"Dog," offers Dad,
        watching Bobo craftily claim
        the front seat
"Friend," Jon tries
        pounding the catcher's mitt I lent him
        for the week while I'm away
"Tent," I say,
        tucking mine tight
        between two old sleeping bags
Soon Jon snaps down his cap
        like a flag at a race
And we're off
        from road to highway
                highway to road
The houses
the billboards
        thin out and vanish
The trees
the mountains
        thicken and grow
And all the while
        tucked tight
        between two sleepy sisters
I whisper, "Tent. Tent. Tent"
        to make sure they get it right

In my tent
  it is dark
    so dark
But I can see
  two greeny gold circles
        of light:
  my fixed and faithful wristwatch
  and a bewildered blinking firefly
    who's trying to have a talk
        with time

I do not know
      this morning
if it is my father
      or the sun
that wakes me first
Both are there
      in my tent
            shining
"Breakfast," Dad declares
Then, "Eggs?" he asks
      pulling one from the air
"Or eggs?"
      coaxing another out of Bobo's ear
I try the same trick
      and come up only with a handful of sunbeams
                  a fistful of fur
"Looking for this?" says Dad
      and there is egg number three
            right under my chin
Then he winks and goes off juggling
      leaving me and the sun
            behind

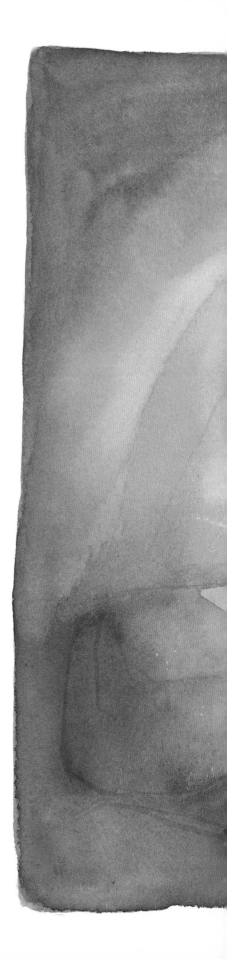

"Don't worry," Mom says
"My great granddad was a Cherokee tracker
    Point me north and I'll get us home"
But still we're lost
    in a forest of blank paper birches
    with no directions on their bark
"North?" I ask
      each chittering chipmunk
      each skittering vole
"Which way's North?" I beg
      the flocking juncos
      the mocking crows
while Mom searches
      for signposts in the shadows
      whereabouts in the wind
In the end it is a man
      face brown and puckered as my catcher's mitt
who pops out of the green and white trees
      like a picture springing from a page
to show us the way
"He looked just like my great granddad"
    I hear Mom say with wonder
    as I run
      fox fast
        to my welcoming tent

Dad's turn tonight
By firelight
    in a voice soft as smoke
he whispers a tale of banshees—
    mournful ghosts with carbuncle eyes
           and electrified hair
    who wail outside a sick man's house
          rattling at the windows
          knocking at the door
    calling "Come, come, your life is done"
Later
by moonlight
I name every night sound
    from the screech owl's watery whistling
    to the katydid's chirr
and tell Bobo I'm glad
    my tent has no windows to rattle
    my tent has no door to knock

There are four of them
    or maybe five
Yodeling softly
    in the darkness
I wake up hiding
    from banshees
Bobo jumps up ready
    for bears
But we stumble
        tumble
    out of my tent
    in time to see
        a gang of raccoons—
            the tips of their ringed tails
            slipping into the trees—
        and an empty sack of dog food
        on the ground
"Your fault," Mom blames Dad
"No, your fault," Dad insists
And the twins howl
    and Bobo barks
    and I laugh
        laugh
            louder than I should
Later
    I hear them again
    far across the river
Bandits boasting
    of their latest catch

One afternoon we watch
    a whole tree-top campground
        of caterpillars
            resting in transparent tents
"One day they'll become moths," Mom says
    though I already know
And then suddenly I imagine
    our whole campground
    tomorrow morning
    all of us coming out of our tents
        people no more
        but something quite changed
And I wonder what it would be like
    to greet a brand-new day
            with brand-new eyes

All day we've been counting houses—
    the squirrel's nest in the oak tree
    the woodpecker's hole in the pine—
Now on the river
    we are so busy following otters
        to find out where they live
  we don't even see the other canoe
        rounding the bend
        don't even notice the man and little girl
        until she wails
            "I want to go home"
        in a voice so loud I swear
        it shakes the sides of our boat
I turn to glimpse her father's frowning face
      wondering what he'll say
Tell her about the water snail
      that wakes up on a lily pad
Tell her about the turtle
      that snoozes in the mud
Most of all, I think
tell her about the people
        who carry tents on our backs
           so every place we go is home
But now we're too far down the river
    for me to hear his answer
Yet from the way Dad is smiling
I know he's heard mine
    though I haven't said a word

With a wooden spoon
>Mom samples supper
>>smacking her lips
>>and muttering strange words I don't understand
>>like *ambrosia* and *nectar of the gods*
Peering into the blue-speckled pot
>I see
>>nothing but plain old baked beans
>>which I never eat at home
"Taste," Mom says
I shake my head
>>not to give in too fast
>>not to find out right away
>if the beans will be changed
>>into something new and delicious
>>the way they always are in this place
"Come on, taste," Mom repeats, "and you'll see"
At last I take a mouthful
>and sure enough it's happened again
"A dish fit for a king," says Mom
And right there
>in front of my tent
>>>my castle
we do a grand little dance
>to celebrate bean magic

Storm!
And my tent
      quivering
      rippling
threatens to float away
like a jellyfish in the sea
Bobo and I huddle inside
      trying to be brave
until a bolt of lightning
      bright and fierce as an electric eel
sizzles across the roaring sky
Then we flee to Mom and Dad's tent
      mudskippers
waiting till the wind is just a whisper
      the rain is just a mist

Last night while the rain drummed
    like a thousand fingers
    on the skin of my tent
I thought about the sun
    and staying dry
Now at high noon the hot dry sun beats
    on my skin
    without a sound
and all I can think about is
    getting wet
"A paradox," Mom calls it
    and leads us all to the place
    where the river pools deep and quiet
    between the rocks
I wade in at once
    crouch neck-high in the coolness
    still as a snail on a stone
Bobo bewildered
    swims tight circles around me
    till tired of the game
    he paddles to the shore
    to dry off in the shade of a willow tree
The twins
    safe in Mom and Dad's hands
    flap their arms
    churn their chubby legs
    scattering newtlets and water boatmen
    sending wide ripples downstream
"A pair o' ducks," laughs Dad
    and he repeats it to make sure
    I get the joke

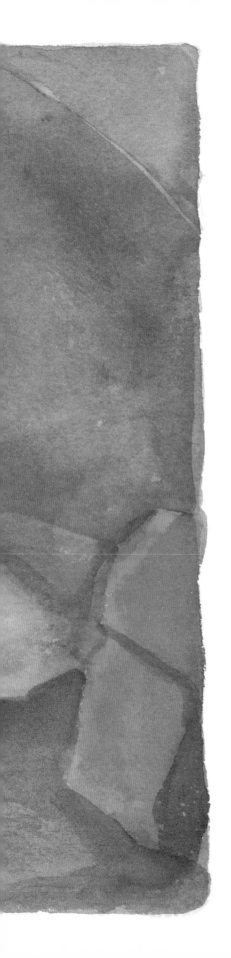

On the day we are leaving
    I find a spider
        spinning a web in my tent
It makes me sad
    to take down her house
        just as I take down mine
But I know she will put up another
        some other place
        just as I will put up mine again
        some other time

On the twins' first birthday
    while everyone celebrates
        with carrot cake and vanilla ice cream
I slip downstairs
    to visit my tent
        hidden away
            like a piece of sun
                in a box
I put my nose inside
    and smell summer
Till Jon
    round as a tomato
        in his red down coat
comes to find me
and we go outside
    to build an igloo
        in the snow